# What I Wish I'd Known Sooner

## TEACHERS

By Carolyn Tomlin

**What I Wish I'd Known Sooner: Teachers**
Carolyn Tomlin
© 2012

ISBN-13: 978-1468194098
Also available in eBook

Cover Design: Hyliian Graphics/Elizabeth E. Little http://hyliian.deviantart.com/
Interior Formatting: Ellen C. Maze www.ellencmaze.com, The Author's Mentor
Photography: ClipArt Factory

Unless otherwise noted, all Scripture quotations taken from the NIV.

Parts of this work were previously published by 1st Books Library as *What I Wish it Hadn't Taken Me So Long to Learn* ©2001, and by Judy Wood Publishing Company ©1999

PRINTED IN THE UNITED STATES OF AMERICA

# Dedication:

For the children
who have touched my life.

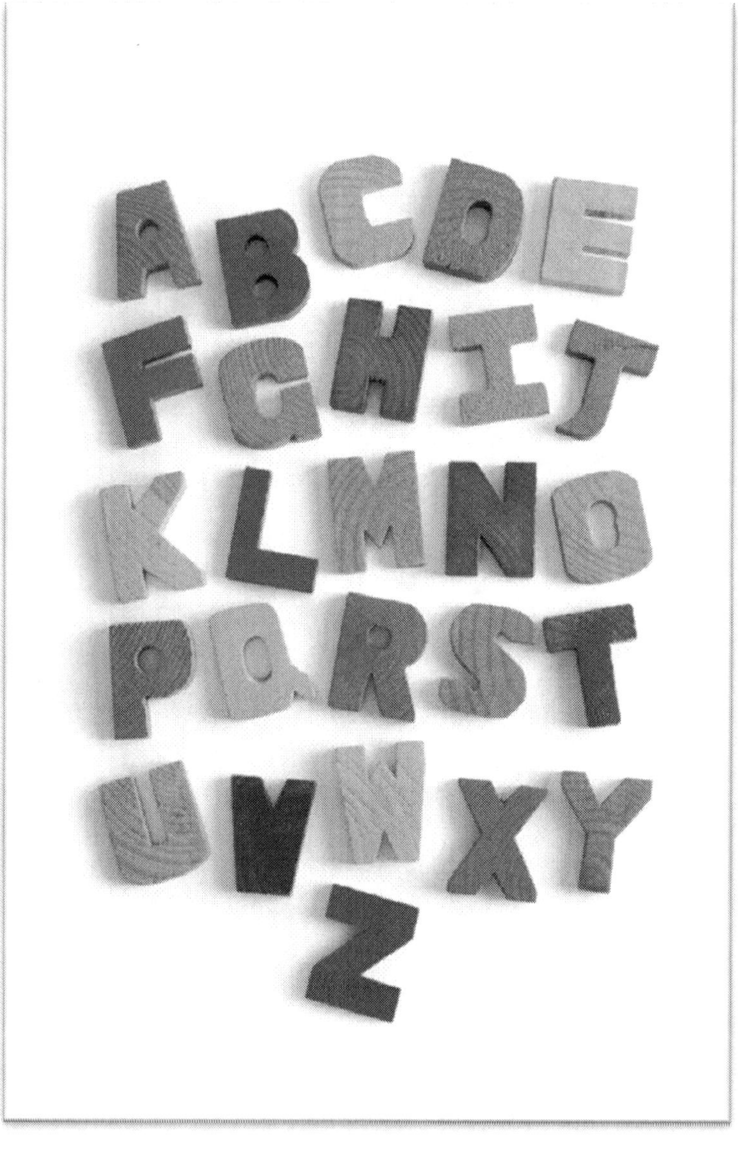
ABCDE
FGHIJ
KLMNO
PQRST
UVWXY
Z

# AUTHOR'S NOTE

The contents of this book focus on topics teachers and educators face throughout the school year. Some are routine. Some required. Others, a matter of choice. Regardless of the situation, if we can laugh at ourselves and with others, it lessens the stress.

For years, I've been interested in how teachers see themselves and how they handle mundane, everyday situations. How do some veteran teachers continue to make learning exciting for both themselves and students? But why do some novice teachers find other employment after the first year or two? What is the difference?

Could we, as career teachers, help those new to the profession, realize that there are essential elements in human growth and development? Could we share what it has taken us a long time to learn?

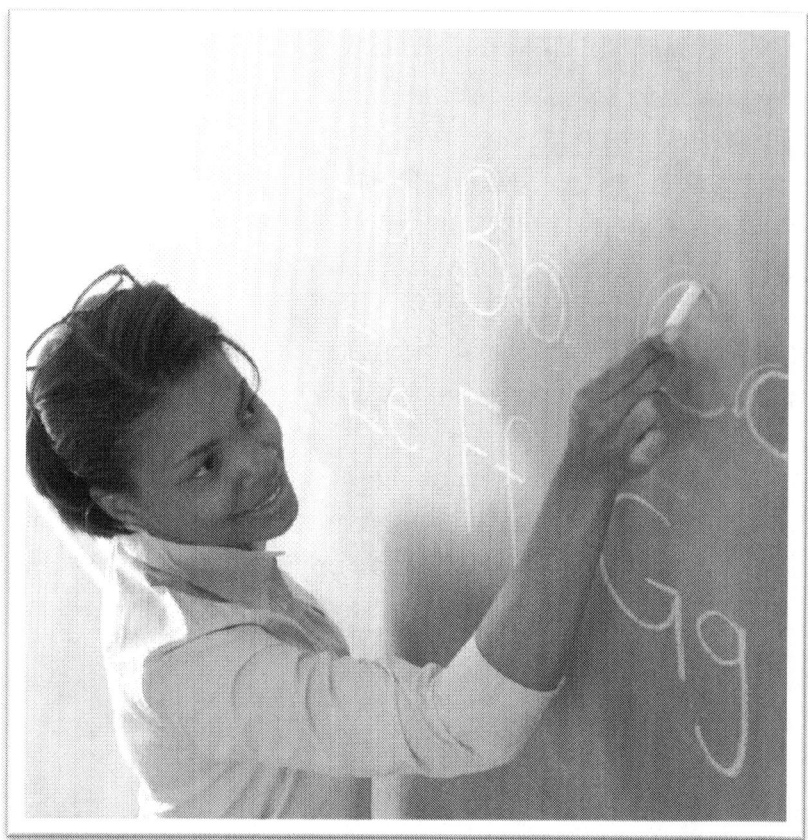

# INTRODUCTION

Teaching is a way of living forever. Bits of wisdom and knowledge we dispense along life's journey—particles of sunshine from those who went before. These, we share with children and youth. And they in turn, pass these fragments on to the next generation. As I discover more, understand more, and reflect more, I often consider how my personal experiences and those from others might be of help to people who have chosen this career.

In addition to bits of wisdom to pass on to other teachers, I believe prayer has a vital place in the lives of those who share their career with children. Regardless of a person's religious affiliation, our faith should be shared with others. And our faith should help us cope with day-by-day problems, as well as daily joys that are part of teaching. Use the prayers as a way to make changes—both the students—and yours.

This book is not mine, entirely. It came from my husband, Matt, who forgot a scheduled speaking engagement. Shortly after he arrived at the meeting, he was introduced as the speaker of the day. Without blinking en eye, he walked to the front, delivered an extemporaneous talk on "What I Wish It Hadn't Taken Me So Long To Learn." The response was tremendous. Others confessed they, too, shared similar feelings.

When I first mentioned this book idea to teachers, many offered tidbits of information from years of being in classrooms. Even after the project was complete—still more material arrived. Just like teaching—there is no end—no finale. However, most of these tidbits of wisdom come from my own classroom and those precious children God entrusted to me each year.

Those of us who love the profession will understand these bits of wisdom. You may even recall parallel experiences. If so, share these with colleagues. Laugh, cry, and rejoice together. How fortunate are those of us who choose to live forever.

# TABLE OF CONTENTS

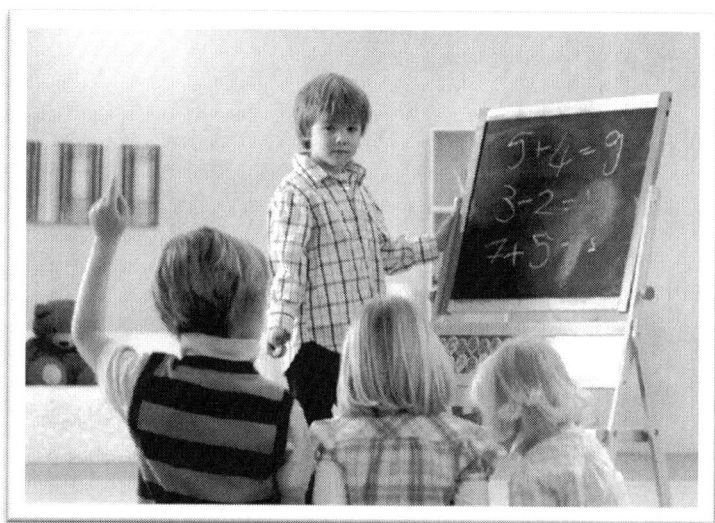

# CHAPTER ONE

## First Day of School

*"The Lord is my strength and my shield; my heart trusts in him, and I am helped. My heart leaps for joy and I will give thanks to him in song."* ~ Psalm 28:7

# Poem for Beginning School

Lord, it's that time of year… again. The summer break just wasn't long enough to complete my "to-do" list.

Did I waste too much time sleeping late?

Did I spend endless hours in personal pleasures?

Why didn't I spend more time in prayer for my upcoming classroom?

Lord, instead of "Beginning of School Blues," help me see this year as a fresh start for wonderful opportunities you may have in store.

Let me face this first day of school with an excitement that shows I genuinely care about each boy and girl. And may my enthusiasm carry over as I greet my students with, "Hey, it's the first day of school! It's going to be a great year!" Amen.

# BITS OF WISDOM:

**1.** Log in ten hours of sleep the night before.

**2.** Wear comfortable walking shoes and cotton socks. (Discard any socks that have even a small hole in the toe. Remember Murphy's Law: Holes grow larger as the day progresses.)

**3.** Take an extra vitamin pill—perhaps two.

**4.** Pack a drinkable lunch. You may not have time to chew.

**5.** Say to yourself, "I will not cry," even when the school bully is assigned to your room.

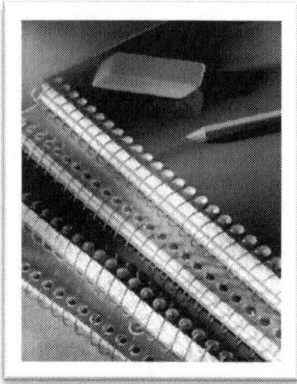

**6.** Try to stay flexible, even when the principal changes your schedule for the fourth time that first day.

**7.** Create a genuine friendship with the school secretary. She may be your best ally in the days ahead.

**8.** Don't count the days remaining in the school year. Or, even until the Christmas holidays—wait a couple of weeks, at least.

**9.** Keep smiling, even though your feet hurt. Children only see your face.

**10.** Have twice as much prepared as you think you'll need.

# CHAPTER TWO

# Open House

*Offer hospitality to one another without grumbling. Each one should use whatever gift he has received to serve others, faithfully administering God's grace in its various forms."* ~ 1 Peter 4:9

# Prayer for the Child of Absentee Parents

Dear Lord, tonight we have Open House at school—a night when parents visit their child's class and meet the teacher.

I see Susan on the fringe of the class watching other children. Like last year, her parents won't be present. Susan's life is different—and she knows it. She sees boys and girls whose parents attend school functions. Those who bake cupcakes for class parties. Those who volunteer to chaperon field trips.

Would Susan trade designer jeans for parents who were home more? Would she gladly exchange a month at an expensive summer camp—just for those small things most kids take for granted?

Lord, give me wisdom. May she accept my offer as I whisper to her, "I don't have a daughter here tonight. Could you pretend you're mine—just for now?" There is no answer. But quietly, a small hand reaches up for mine. Amen.

# BITS OF WISDOM

**1.** Prior to open house, remove any fish floating "belly-up."

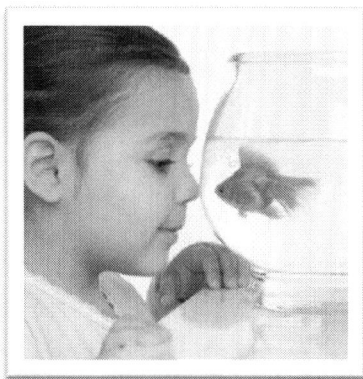

**2.** Check on the hamster. "Is he really asleep—or has he gone to his great reward?"

**3.** Flush all commodes if you're in a self-contained classroom.

**4.** Never say to senior adults, "It's so good to see grandparents interested in their grandchildren's school." They may be the child's biological parents!

**5.** Hide clutter in your room. Store it in your car until the event is over.

**6.** Break the ice by offering soft drinks, coffee, and simple cookies. Wipe up splashes of cola and pick up crumbs later.

**7.** Show a genuine concern for all parents and extended family members, cousins, and more cousins, who visit your room. But, keep an eye on the cookie plate.

**8.** Make a "wish list" for classroom supplies usually purchased from your paycheck. Ask each parent to choose one item from the list.

**9.** Lessen the stress by playing soft background music.

# CHAPTER THREE

# Parent-Teacher Conference

*But the fruit of the Spirit is love, joy, peace, patience, kindness, goodness, faithfulness, gentleness, and self-control.* ~ Galatians 5:22

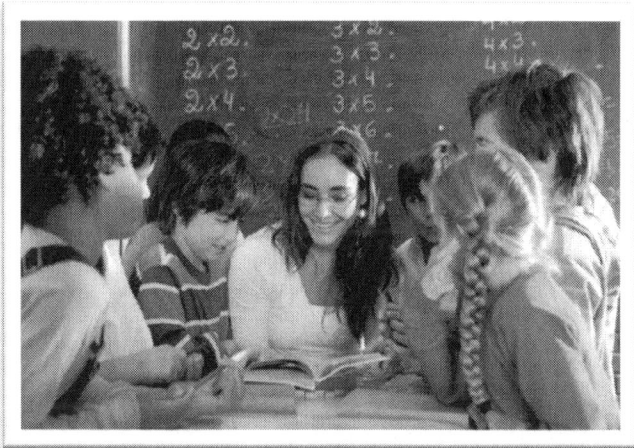

# Prayer for Meeting New Families

Lord, help me today as I greet new parents. I see a few familiar faces, but for the most part—these are strangers.

These parents trust me with their precious children. It's up to me to teach not only academics, but character building, self-confidence, pride in one's work, and hundreds of other things.

May I not fail any child.

May I see the potential in each boy and girl.

And may I have the family's support at home as I do my best at school.

Help me think before I speak.

May I have self-control in everything I do and say.

But just for now, Lord, help me get through this first Parent-Teacher Conference!

Amen.

# BITS OF WISDOM

**1.** Remember your mother's advice: If you can't say something good about someone—say nothing at all.

**2.** Begin with positive words. Look for small accomplishments such as, "Your child can eat more broccoli than anyone in the class!"

**3.** Place individual folders on each child's desk. Remember your seating arrangement. Children will know.

**4.** Try to schedule blocks of time. Place a chair outside your door for early arrivals or drop-ins so you may speak privately with parents.

**5.** Refer to your notes about each child's strengths and weakness. Have an over-abundance of positive remarks.

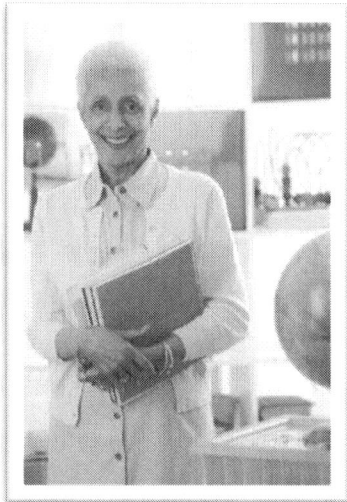

**6.** Make every parent a classroom volunteer. List activities for parents who work during the school day.

**7.** Draw the parent into the conversation. What does their child say about school?

**8.** Be organized. Place each handout in a separate folder. Color-coded paper helps if dropped.

**9.** If a parent says their child is unhappy at school, could *you* be the problem?

**10.** Realize that parents know their child better than you do.

# CHAPTER FOUR

# Bus Duty

*"Do not be anxious about anything, but in everything, by prayer and petition, with thanksgiving, present your requests to God." ~ Philippians 4:6*

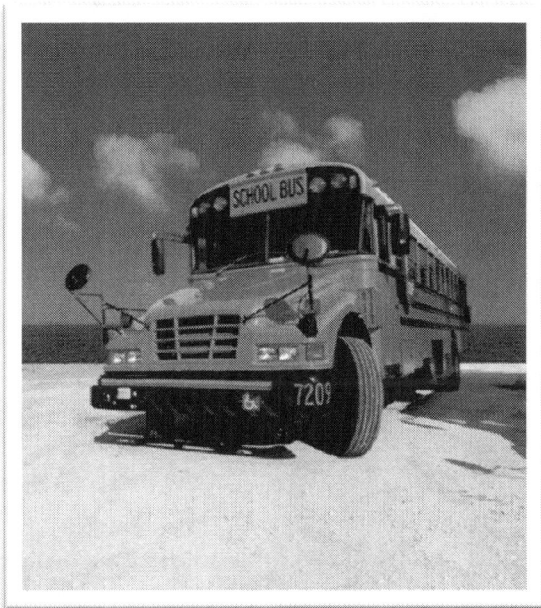

# Prayer for an Extra Long Day

Lord, it's going to be a long day. In fact, a very long week.

After teaching thirty students from 8:00 a.m. to 3:30 p.m., now I have late bus duty.

Help me realize these boys and girls are tired, too. Like teachers, small children also grow weary.

May I challenge these second bus load students with activities that will rest their minds and relax their bodies.

Give me patience, Lord.

Help me remember what it was like to be a child myself.

But…we're all "SO" ready to go home!

Amen.

# BITS OF WISDOM

**1.** If a child misses the bus and you have to drive them home—get more information than, "I live on a hill and there's a big tree in the yard."

**2.** If a bus breaks down before the second load, realize you may have a two-hour wait.

**3.** If a child ties his shoe laces together in several hard knots and the bus is called, get the scissors.

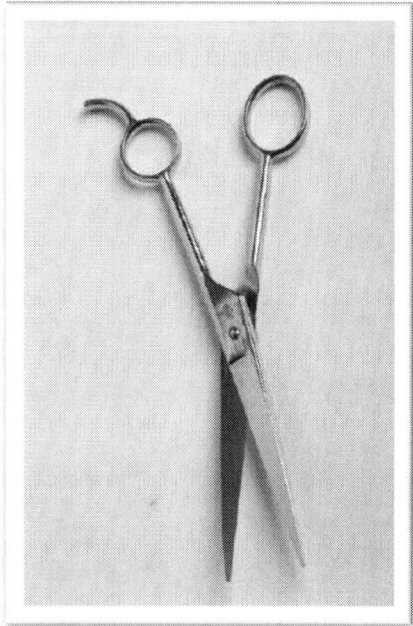

**4.** A law of nature states: After a child puts on his heavy coat, gloves, book bag, and the bus is called, he always has to use the bathroom.

**5.** If a child says, "I'm not riding my regular bus home. I'm going to Grandma's house," call Grandma before the regular bus leaves the school grounds.

**6.** If a frantic parent reports their child did not get off the bus at home, check the bus garage for a sleeping youngster.

**7.** Enforce this rule, "No Dogs Allowed on Buses," even if Mary's lamb came to school.

**8.** Keep a list of students' bus numbers at your house.

**9.** Pair a new student with a responsible person for the bus ride home. Speak to the driver about his new rider.

# CHAPTER FIVE

# Holiday and Seasons

*"There is a time for everything and a season for every activity under heaven."*~ Ecclesiastes 2:14

# Prayer for Finding Teachable Moments in Celebrating Holidays

Lord, my calendar is circled marking all the holidays our school celebrates. I think there are more today than when I was a youngster.

We honor brave men and women who helped make our country great, traditional religious holidays and local days for our school system.

Please help me remember how it was to be a child and the excitement those days bring.

May I stay focused on the curriculum guide while still allowing fun activities.

You know that young children learn best through their senses. And you told stories to connect with people.

Of course, there's another reason I still love holidays: *School is out!*

Amen.

# BITS OF WISDOM

**I.** Even if the Easter holiday is near—never wear a bunny suit all day!

**2.** Around Halloween, don't drive to school wearing a witch costume!

**3.** Realize the second-hand Christmas gift wrapped in newspaper may be a gift you'll always treasure.

**4.** Don't bring a pet turkey to school the day before Thanksgiving holidays.

**5.** Move the students in the same direction around the May Pole.

**6.** If a student brings you a box of Valentine candy with a few pieces missing, it's okay to eat it. Avoid peanuts from which the chocolate has been sucked off.

**7.** Celebrate an unexpected snow. Grab coats and play outside. Catch snowflakes with your tongue. Make snow angels in the yard. Add milk and sugar to cups of fresh snow for a special treat. You'll create memories not found in books.

**8.** Observe Black History Month by recognizing people in your community who have contributed to your school.

**9.** Treat those children whose families do not observe traditional holidays with kindness and respect. Plan another activity that is equally exciting.

**10.** Praise the child who colors a St. Patrick "leprechaun" dark purple and Santa Claus a bright yellow. She may be our next Picasso.

**11.** Advise parents to omit names on children's valentines for non-readers. Otherwise, you call 625 names for 25 children who bring each friend a card.

**12.** If your school allows two parties per year, combine the other holidays you want to observe with social studies.

**13.** Watch for snakes in the grass during May Day celebrations.

**14.** Be thankful for gifts made from loving hands.

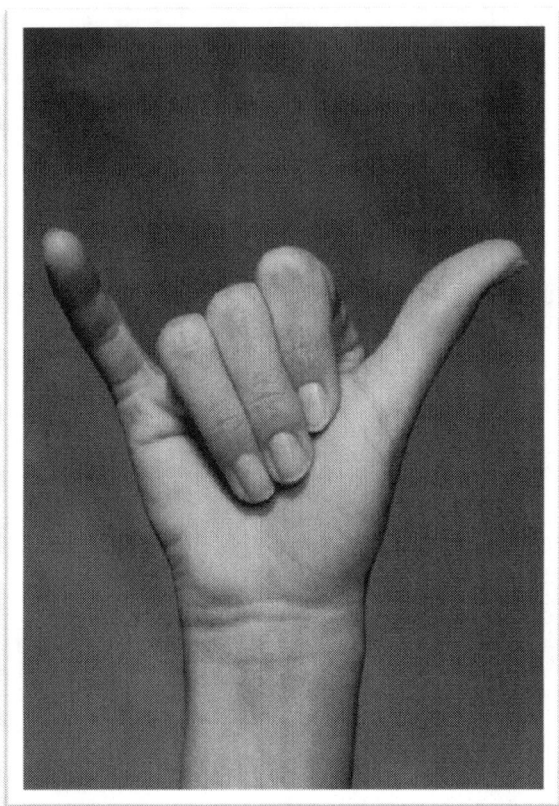

# CHAPTER SIX

# Sick Days and Substitute Teachers

*"Cast your cares on the Lord and he will sustain you;*
*he will never let the righteous fall."*
~Psalm 55:22

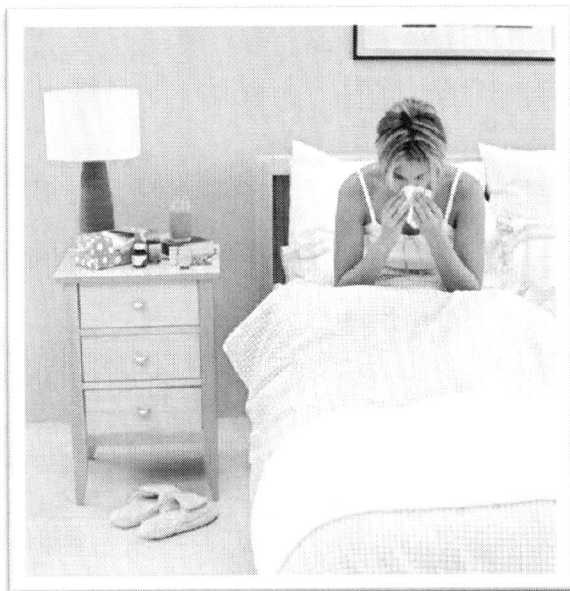

# Prayer for My Substitute Teacher

Lord, my students have a substitute teacher today. I realize it's a challenge to walk into another classroom and pick up where the regular teacher left off.

Please help her find my lesson plans and the curriculum guide.

May she understand that Ashley's shyness requires a sensitive heart.

Help her tell the difference early in the day between Joey and Johnny, my identical twins. They've been known to switch clothes, work, and seats several times when I'm away—thus causing constant confusion for the sub.

And may there be no fire or tornado alarms while I'm absent.

Dear Lord, please help her keep my students safe and give her patience until I return.

Amen.

# BITS OF WISDOM

**1.** After you call a substitute the night before, never answer a ringing phone early the next morning.

**2.** Never tell your principal which hospital your surgery is scheduled if you're on a committee for school-wide goals.

**3.** Request a personal skateboard if your leg is still in a cast and you've used all your sick days.

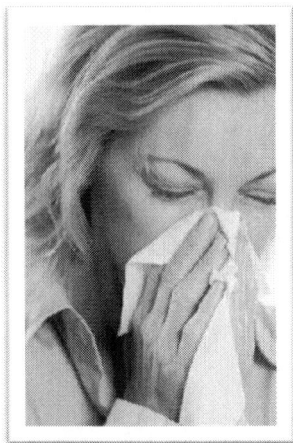

**4.** Encourage teachers to sign a petition that states: Any teacher with a temperature of over 105° Fahrenheit is to be sent home immediately.

**5.** Place in large red letters on your daily plan book: Substitute teachers, please do not cover more than two pages in Algebra II per day-even if students insist.

**6.** If you have identical twins in two separate classes, make sure you have someone who can easily recognize the one in your room. (Twins have been known to change rooms when the substitute teacher arrives.)

**7.** If students remark after you return from sick leave, "I wish our substitute teacher was back. She let us watch videos all day!" prepare to re-teach.

**8.** Place a recording of whale sounds on your desk if students become too aggressive for the substitute teacher.

**9.** Realize it's often easier to come to school sick than to catch up when you return.

**10.** Stress that the homework hotline does not apply the day after surgery.

# CHAPTER SEVEN

# Faculty Meetings and Colleagues

*"Do not judge, or you too will be judged. For in the same way you judge others, you will be judged, and with the measure you use, it will be measured to you."*
~ Matthew 7:1-2

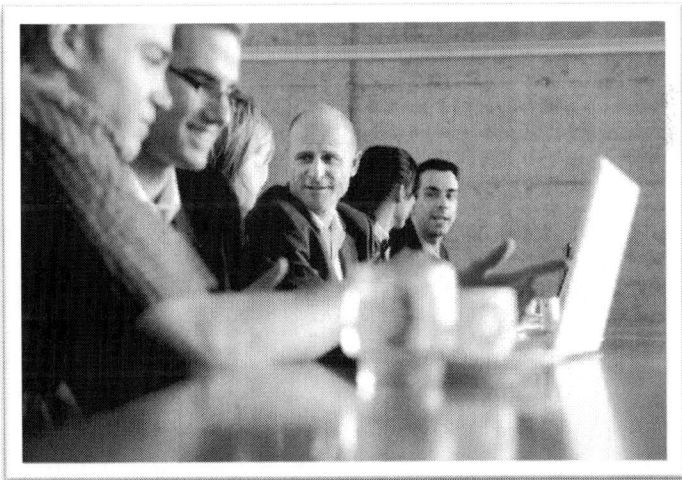

# Prayer for the Teacher I Do Not Like

Lord, is it just me? Why do I have a problem with this teacher? Maybe it's because she yells at her students. Or, perhaps it's because she comes in late several times a week? Or when there is a fund-raiser, she always has something else planned.

If I ask myself, "Would I want my own child to be in this atmosphere all day? The answer is a clear, "NO!"

Help me see her strengths and not her weaknesses. Would I change my opinions of her if I knew her better?

Lord, help me reach out to someone who may be lonely—someone who may be burned out in this career—someone who has health problems, unknown but to You.

And, help me remember to include her in my daily prayers.

Amen.

# BITS OF WISDOM

**1.** When the principal says, "This after-school faculty meeting won't take long," be prepared to stay until dark.

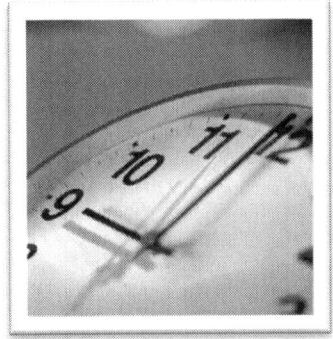

**2.** When the faculty meeting is over and the principal says, "Does *anyone* have *anything* for the good of the cause?" don't answer.

**3.** There's no such thing as a free lunch for the faculty. Someone pays.

**4.** A slow-cooker is no excuse for leaving the faculty meeting early to check on the evening meal.

**5.** Never look the principal in the eye when she asks for volunteers on a school committee. Tie your shoe, or drop your pencil and retrieve it.

**6.** When your school plans a fund-raiser, be the first to volunteer. The best jobs go fast.

**7.** Avoid the squeaky chair during a faculty meeting. You get more attention than you want.

**8.** Realize that having a coughing spell and having to leave early only works a couple of times.

**9.** Never play tic-tac-toe with a colleague during faculty meetings. They may be promoted to supervisor next year.

**10.** If you're in a long faculty meeting, don't tap your wrist watch on the table to see if it's still running.

**11.** Never bring a cell phone or pager into a faculty meeting.

**12.** If your feet swell, never kick your shoes off under the table. You may regret it!

# CHAPTER EIGHT

# Discipline

*"Trust in the Lord and do good..."*
~ Psalm 37:3

# Prayer for the Child Who Needs Extra Attention

Lord, Manuel did it again!

This is the third time this week he's been fighting. And Manuel is at least a head taller than his classmates—plus twenty pounds heavier.

He always says, "It wasn't my fault! He started it!" But I was there each time—and I know Manuel is to blame.

What am I going to do?

How can I change his behavior without hurting his strong-willed spirit?

First, I gave him time-out; he loved it.

Next, I assigned extra work; he completed it quickly.

Then I heard your still, small voice that said, *"Perhaps Manuel just needs some extra love."* As my plan isn't working, I'm trying your suggestion, Lord.

Why do we try to do things by ourselves instead of turning to you in prayer?

Today, I asked Manuel, "Do you think you could help me with something?"

His eyes lit up. "I… guess so," he said.

"I need you to be a buddy to a new boy who's coming into our room. Do you think you could do this?"

That was two weeks ago. Today, Manuel has become a model student—simply because he felt needed. No longer does he need attention from inappropriate behavior. I've learned to "catch him being good."

Lord, how did you know this would work?

Thank you, Lord, for teaching me a lesson in trust and making a difference in my classroom, Manuel, and especially, me. Amen.

# BITS OF WISDOM

**I.** Have you noticed that sometimes there is more violence in classrooms than on television?

**2.** Desktop publishing is not when a child takes a crayon and marks all over his desk.

**3.** An hour of video games won't count as "time-out."

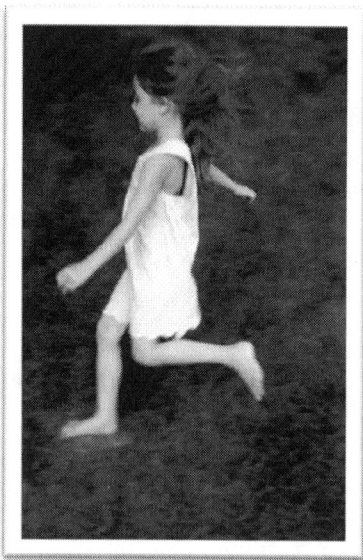

**4.** Gently mention to an educator who gave a speech on discipline that there is a big difference between the terms *capital punishment* and *corporal punishment.*

**5.** Running short stretches once an hour releases stress for over-active students. Works for teachers, too.

**6.** When you must discipline a student, envision your own children or grandchildren. How would you want them to be treated?

**7.** Catch students being good.

**8.** Believe in yourself. Students will follow.

**9.** Share your lunch time with the "Student of the Day."

**10.** Be big enough to apologize when you're wrong.

*For where your treasure is, there your heart will be also.* ~ Matthew 6:21

# CHAPTER NINE

# Assorted Gems

*"I can do everything through him who gives me strength."* ~ Philippians 4:13

# Prayer for Rainy Days

Lord, is that rain I hear?

Please… not another day of staying indoors. After all—it's the third day this week. Don't you realize that active students need physical activity each day? And after being outside to run off that boundless energy, they return refreshed and ready to learn.

Give me patience as their restlessness grows.

May I maintain my sanity until the dismissal bell. Then I'll pass them on to parents who face another afternoon of cooped up children on a rainy afternoon. Amen.

# BITS OF WISDOM

**1.** Blackberry stain on a child's face doesn't *always* mean the child is guilty of eating the teacher's jelly donut.

**2.** If a child says, "I wish you were my Momma," take it as your best compliment of the day.

**3.** Realize that soup stays on a spoon better if crackers are crumbled in the bowl. (Learned from a father's note after I gave a lesson on good table manners.)

**4.** Some of the cute sayings young children announce are best not repeated. (Learned from asking a kindergarten child to identify body parts. When I said, "Point to your waist," the child, not knowing how, but wanting to respond, said, "I must be made like Grandma. She doesn't have one, either!")

**5.** Instead of saying to a student, "This won't work. Your answer is wrong!" Say, "Could we try it another way?"

**6.** Realize that children see things differently from adults. (Learned when taking a group of kindergarten children on a nature walk and seeing a mocking bird. I said, "This particular bird can repeat songs others sing." A freckled-face youngster looked up and said, "Do you think he knows 'Jesus Love Me'?")

**7.** Check bathroom stalls before leaving for the day. Young children's feet are not visible when sitting on the potty.

**8.** If a child leaves liquid glue open in her book bag and the bus is called, pretend you don't see it. Announce to all children, "Have your parents check your book bags tonight!"

**9.** You struggle to pull on a child's rubber boots, and when you finally get them on, the child says: "These aren't my boots." Then, you manage to eventually get them off. Don't get upset when the child says, "They're my little brother's boots. He let me wear them today!"

**10.** Chocolate candy at 2:00 each afternoon has kept many a teacher from early retirement.

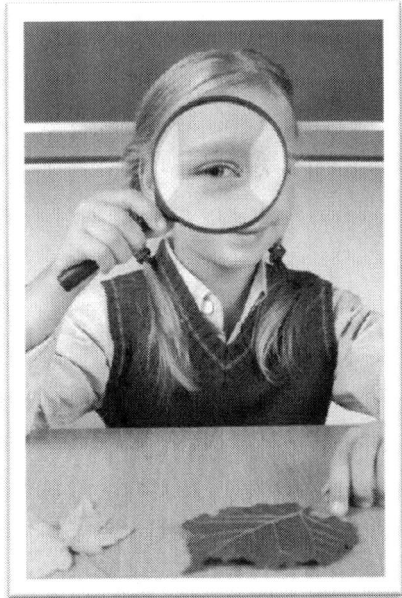

**11.** If you room lacks a window, paint a mural.

**12.** Discipline your body functions to "before" and "after" school only.

**13.** A turtle only moves forward when he comes out of his shell. What about you?

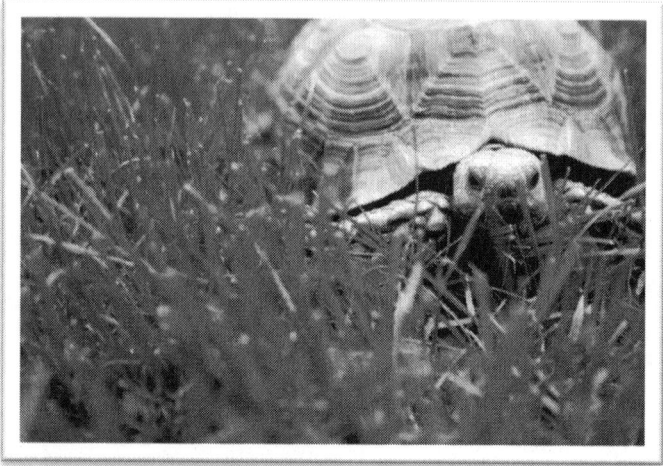

**14.** Ask not what your school can do for you. Ask what you can do for your students.

**15.** If you've been dieting and children draw you as a "stick figure," reward them.

**16.** Realize students today have more history to learn than the present generation of teachers. We've lived it!

**17.** Find something you really enjoy doing to relieve the stress of the classroom. You'll feel better about yourself and it will show in your teaching as you relate to students.

**18.** Realize that intelligence is measured in many ways. Even the 5-year-old special education student who cooked his own breakfast, missed the bus, and walked with his dog the three miles to school.

**19.** When a child says, "I don't have enough fingers to count to fifteen!" offer her yours.

**20.** Realize that small children see things from a different viewpoint than adults. Some days it's only knees and legs—unless you stoop to their level.

**21.** Be grateful for today's teaching salary. Eighty years ago, my mother taught four grades in a two-room school for $60.00 a month. That included building a fire to heat the building, making a pot of soup for lunch and keeping the room clean.

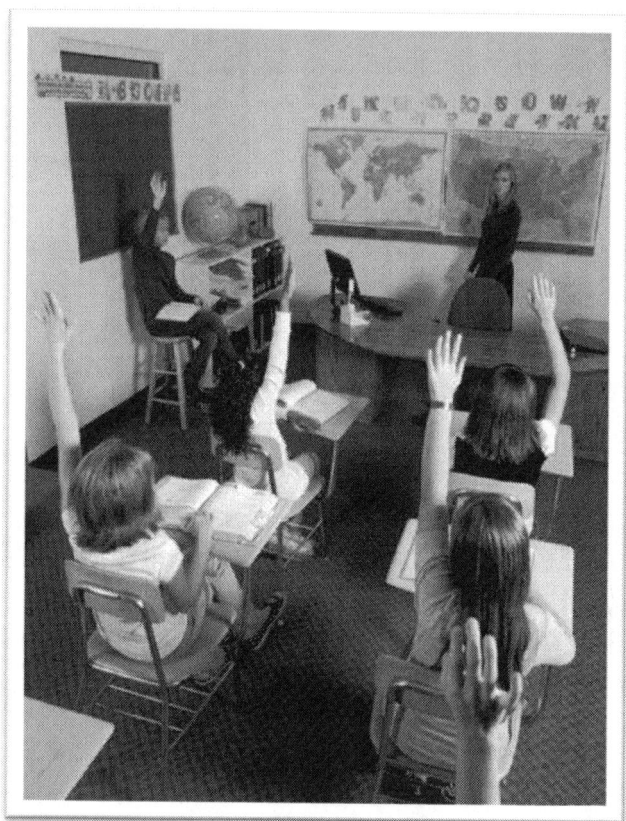

# ADDITIONAL PRAYERS

*Hear my prayer, LORD;*
*listen to my cry for mercy.*
*When I am in distress, I call to you,*
*because you answer me.*
*~ Psalm 86: 6-7*

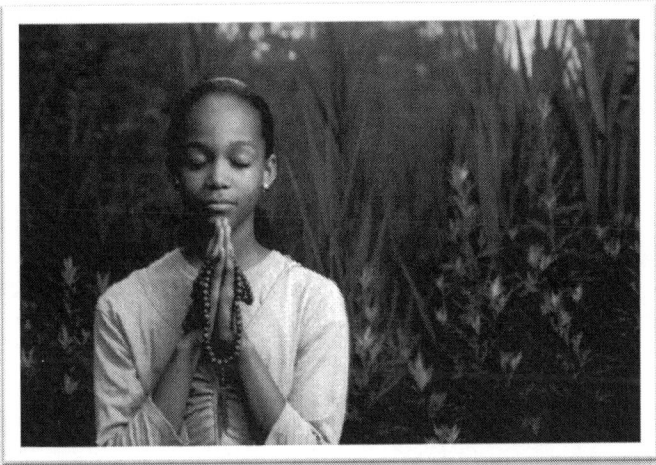

# Prayer for the Child with a Terminal Illness and for Children with Special Needs

Lord, I watch David as he struggles to keep up with his friends. It's no secret—the child has AIDS, the silent killer that snatches its victims in a horrible illness. Through no fault of his own, he is dying.

I've been so proud of my class this year. Because of David's illness we're studying about new diseases that affect mankind.

Changes have occurred in each boy and girl. There's Todd who goes by David's home each afternoon to play indoor games. Karen tutors when he doesn't feel like attending school. Another student, who was afraid to sit near him at first, now says, "Helping others is a gift only 'I' can give." And Joseph wants so

become a scientist when he grows up. Why? To discover a cure for Acquired Immune Deficiency. Then, he can help thousands of others like his friend, David.

Lord, David could have been placed in another room. But, you and all your wisdom, knew my needs and those of my students. Thank you for sending David to teach us. Amen.

# Prayer for the Child from a Broken Home

Lord, he comes to school with downcast eyes. He can't seem to concentrate. He doesn't seem to care, anymore. The rumor must be true—his parents have filed for divorce.

Help me as I guide him over the days and weeks to come. Will it make it easier on him if I say, *You're not alone? That 50% of kids live with single parents?* Or, that I say, *You'll see your Dad on holidays and two weeks during the summer?* I doubt that will bring a smile to his small face.

Give me wisdom, Lord. Help me convey the message that the divorce wasn't his fault. That nothing he did—or did not do—would have made a difference. And may our classroom be one of healing for wounds both seen, and unseen. Amen.

# Prayer for the Child in the Middle

Lord, he's not the oldest, he's not the youngest. He's Mario, the one in the middle of three kids in his family. Is that the reason why some days he insists he's a "baby" and other days he rules the class?

Yet, day-by-day, I see improvement. (To be honest, some days it's difficult to measure.) Thank you, Lord, for small things, like giving me twenty-four students this year. Twenty-four, being an even number, has no room for "middles."

Lord, help me teach Mario and other middle children that life has challenges. And challenges help us grow. Amen

# Prayer for the Child Placed With a Foster Family

Lord, bless Tekika, my student. This small girl has been placed with a wonderful Christian family. You, in your wisdom, were part of this decision. This husband and wife team has a home where Christ is present and where love abounds. They've already helped so many children.

May this precious child who has never known security—find peace.

One who has gone to bed hungry—have nourishment.

One who has seen enough violence to last a lifetime—find unconditional love.

You, of all people, Lord, understand. Help this family provide a home that will become a role model for her as an adult. Amen.

# THE END

# ABOUT THE AUTHOR

Carolyn Tomlin has published over 3,600 magazine articles in the field of education, parenting, gardening, travel, pets, crafts and cooking. She lives in Jackson, Tennessee with her husband, Matt, and a Pomeranian puppy named Rocky. They are the parents of two adult children and six grandchildren.

Working with Denise George, she is the co-founder and teacher of "Boot Camp for Christian Writers." By teaching participants to write-to-publish, hundreds of people have become published writers. This personal ministry is making a difference in the lives of others.

She is a frequent speaker for women's ministry, grant seminars, teacher training and writing classes.

Tomlin is the co-author of *The Secret Holocaust Diaries: The Untold Story of Nonna Bannister*, published by Tyndale. This award winning book has been published in the German and Norwegian translations. Other books written by the author and published by the Judy Wood Publishing Company include: *From the Cat's Point of View; A Parent's Guide to Summer Survival, African Americans Who Made a Difference, Tall Tales or True Tales* (with Denise George) and *365 Email Questions and Answers for Students* (with Veronica Coulston). Published by the Women's Missionary Union is *More Alike Than Different* and *First Steps in Missions. Be a Math Tutor,* a math handbook for students was published by the Frank Schaffer Company.
**Email the author at Carolyn.tomlin@yahoo.com.**

But the fruit of the spirit is love, joy, peace, patience, kindness,
goodness, faithfulness, gentleness, and self-control.
~ Galatians 5:22-23

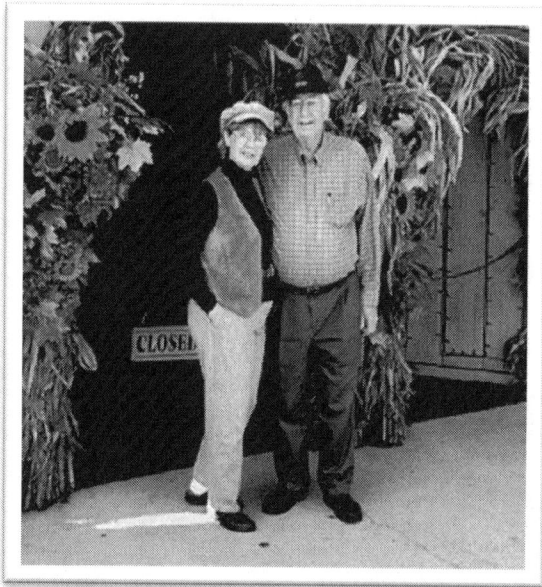

The Author and her husband, Matt